ADVANCE PRAISE FOR *LEADERSHIP IN VERSE*

"*In* Leadership in Verse, *sage philosopher poet John Baldoni captures hope, spirit, purpose, and soul, and connects them to leadership, reflection, example, and practice. At once gently informative and deeply honest, John's thoughtful perspective on humanity and leadership shines through the pages of this one-of-a-kind book of poems for leaders and followers.*"
Sarah McArthur, Editor in Chief, Apex Award-winning *Leader to Leader* Journal

"*In* Leadership in Verse, *John Baldoni reveals what many leadership books miss: the soul of the leader. These poems invite reflection and recommitment to what matters most for anyone who leads another. It's a beautiful, brave contribution to the field of poetry and leadership science. Bravo, John!*"
Adrian Gostick, New York Times bestselling author of *All In* and *Leading with Gratitude*

"*Leadership in Verse offers a fresh and unexpectedly powerful way to explore what it really means to lead. Through poetry, John Baldoni captures the truths leaders often feel but rarely articulate — burnout, grace, humility, courage, and the inner tensions of decision-making. His words invite us to pause, reflect, and reconnect with the deeper purpose behind our leadership. This collection is a gift: a reminder that leadership is not just something we do — it's who we become through awareness, compassion, and conscious choice.*"
Brenda Bence, Thinkers50 Coaching Legend | Hall of Fame Speaker
Author of *Would YOU Want to Work for YOU?*

"*The grind of work seems fallow ground for poetry but in the imagination of John Baldoni it becomes fodder for insight and inspiration.* Leadership in Verse *reveals the mental anguish leaders experience alongside the behaviors we can exert to effect positive change. Baldoni augments the poems with stories about inspirational figures whose lives give us all hope.* Leadership in Verse *is a book every leader will want in their resource library.*"
Dr. Greg Williams, The Master Negotiator

"*In John Baldoni's latest book of leadership poetry, he shines a light on the challenges and absurdities of organizational life, while acknowledging the humanity of the people onstage. John's compassion and decency are amply evident in* Leadership in Verse, *which I recommend to anyone who could use some support from a tough-minded coach.*"
Ed Batista, Executive Coach

Act with Courage

Know your values.

Make the tough choice the right choice.

Set the right example by living by your values.

Act resolutely under pressure.

Recognize the bravery of others.

Courage is the ability to remain resolute in the face of crisis, show bravery and persevere in adversity.

ALSO BY JOHN BALDONI

Golf Lessons: Chips, Chunks and Cheers (2025)

Grace Under Pressure: Leading Through Change and Crisis (2023)

Grace Notes: Leading in an Upside-Down World (2021)

Grace: A Leader's Guide to a Better Us (2019)

Moxie: The Secret to Bold and Gutsy Leadership (2015)

The Leader's Guide to Speaking with Presence: How to Project Confidence, Conviction, and Authority (2013)

The Leader's Pocket Guide: Indispensable Tools, Tips, and Techniques for Any Situation (2012)

Lead with Purpose: Giving Your Organization a Reason to Believe in Itself (2011)

12 Steps to Power Presence: How to Assert Your Authority to Lead (2010)

Lead Your Boss: The Subtle Art of Managing Up (2009)

Lead by Example: 50 Ways Great Leaders Inspire Results (2008)

How Great Leaders Get Great Results (2005)

Great Motivation Secrets of Great Leaders (2004)

Great Communication Secrets of Great Leaders (2003)

180 Ways to Walk the Motivation Talk (2002), co-authored with Eric L. Harvey

Personal Leadership: Taking Control of Your Work Life (2001)

180 Ways to Walk the Leadership Talk (2000)

DEDICATION

To the memory of my parents

Martha Watt Baldoni

and

L. P. Baldoni M.D.

Your lessons inspired me every day.

Leadership in Verse

- POEMS & STORIES BY -

JOHN BALDONI

CONTENTS

Poetry is the art of getting to the heart of the matter.

It gives structure to ideas that are often overlooked or ignored, but nonetheless must be explored.

Poetry puts thoughts into verse in ways that make tough subjects approachable and accessible.

Leadership, too, is about reaching the heart as well as the mind.

Leaders are called upon to address challenging issues and act with candor and courage to address them.

Poetry can be a siren song for action.

Leadership can be those songs put into action.

PROLOGUE

Let's be honest. This was not a book I had intended to write.

After publishing fifteen books on leadership, including one collection of leadership reflections, I had said all I could say. Besides, my new avocation—in addition to piano and golf—was poetry. That's where I display my creative writing skills. And again, being honest, I could never find a way to write about leadership in the form of poetry (apart from my collection of ChatBot poems on the topic).

Then I realized that I had some things I could say differently, perhaps in a more heartfelt way. I started writing about grace, and readers and listeners liked it. So why don't I explore stories? I have hundreds that, with the proper application, might be worthy of a poetic twist.

And, being one who has spent over three decades writing about leadership—as well as teaching and coaching it—I know I still have some things to say.

I call this new volume *Leadership in Verse.* The title could be interpreted in two ways. Leadership Inverse—when everything you do seems the opposite of what you should do, or as written, Leadership IN Verse—aspirations and behaviors put into meter.

The volume you hold in your hands is divided into three parts:

What We See are observations of management that we see around us in good times and in bad.

How We Act is a set of leadership thoughts and actions that come in handy in times of stress.

Stories to Inspire is a collection of stories about women and men who have inspired me to write because they exemplify what it means to lead with strength, bravery, and heart. None are perfect —just like me—but all are worthy of exploration.

Leadership in Verse represents a new chapter for me, and I hope readers find it worthy of exploration and learning.

Lead on!

❋

Employ Mercy

Mercy is a virtue. It is a practice of better living for a better us and a better self. Thinking of mercy naturally raises the issue of how to act with it.

Act with respect toward others. View others with an open heart. Give them the benefit of the doubt before drawing conclusions.

Demonstrate compassion. We all make mistakes. Show some understanding. Act for the good of others.

Resolve to do better next time. There will be times when you slip into bad habits, lashing out at others, showing them no mercy. Apologize to those you have wronged and move forward.

Mercy to ourselves. The author Thomas Merton, a Catholic monk, grounded much of his writing on mercy. "We are not all weak in the same spots, and so we supplement and complete one another, each one making up in himself for the lack in another."

We must accept finite disappointment, but we must never lose infinite hope.
—Martin Luther King, Jr.

What We See

Leadership is about making a positive difference.
The difference becomes obvious when we look around at the world as it is,
rather than how we wish it to be.
Too often we see what we want to see without seeing what is truly before us.

BURNOUT

Gnawing emptiness pervades.
Fatigue without perceived exertion.
Endless hours of sameness.
Hour upon hour.
"It's like being drunk," they say.
If so, there's no comfort. No high.
Just exhaustion.
What took an hour may take a half-day,
Including time spent staring.
Worse. A loss of what and why?
What am I doing,
And why am I am doing it?
Motions for the sake of motion.
Burnout.

THEY SAID

They said:
It's the product.
It's the customer.
It's the competition.
It's the people.
It's the culture.
It's management.
It's the system.

But I said no.
It's me.
I am responsible for
Improving the product.
Serving the customer.
Beating the competition.
Teaching our people.
Nurturing our culture.
Improving our management.
Being OUR leader.

RUNNING DRY

"And then," he said, "our funding dried up.

"No more cash flowing.

"Had to lay off half the staff.

"More even if you count the part-timers, too.

"Canceled contracts right and left.

"It got so that when our bank called I had to leave the room.

"Let 'em talk to the finance guy.

"Our lease was about up and no way we could renew.

"Figured we'd all work from home, you know.

"Crazy to do when you really don't have a plan,

"Actually we had a plan—too many plans. That was the problem.

"No real direction. Except going down, down, down.

"Running dry," he said aloud in the office.

Silent. Dry. Empty.

THE SPEAKER

He took the stage, and mouse-like, scurried toward the podium.
He began speaking before he reached his destination.
He raced to get the words out,
Almost as if he didn't want anyone to hear what he had to say.
Too bad.
He's a bright fellow, and off stage, lively and even engaging.
On stage he freezes, until he can free himself from the podium
And scurry back to his seat.
Before anyone noticed he was there.

THE WINDOW

He found himself looking out the window
Not out of boredom, but because he could not stand to look at the two people
seated in front of him.
They were his responsibility, he reminded himself
As he heard them bicker back and forth
About what he had forgotten.
Their contempt for each other was fueled by the size of their egos.
Big, bold, and intolerant.
He should fire the both of them, he thought.
But then he would have to hire someone else,
And that would cut into his time looking out the window.

THE NEXT GUY

"Joe's a bright fellow," she explained. "Really knows his stuff."

"Only trouble is that no one likes him.

"He can be rude, loud, and arrogant.

"He also does not like to listen to anyone else.

"What can you do to help him?" She asked earnestly.

I told her that I didn't do personality transplants.

"Well, he's in line to be our next CEO," she added.

Perhaps, I thought, you might want to polish your resume.

"He's really not that bad, if you stay out of his way."

CLICK CLICK

"And here you can see the differential between…"
He stopped mid-sentence.
His PowerPoint slides had stopped advancing.
"Give me a minute," he said, nervously pushing the advance slide button.
As the seconds ticked—he sweated, becoming red-faced.
"Damn it," he bellowed, "I told my guys my computer was choking."
Actually, it was he who was losing his breath, as quickly as he was his cool.
Whatever he was presenting did not matter.
His message was simple, I am a victim.
He paced back and forth, hoping that something,
Someone would come to his rescue.
Alone on the stage, holding his clicker.

BLEMISHED CHARACTER

It starts fresh and green,
Not yet ripe.
In days or so, it will be yellow.
First bright and firm to the touch.
The yellow hues ripen into vibrancy
The fruit it bears inside awaits the peeling.
The flesh is still firm and sweet.
In a day or so, or maybe more,
It may be too sweet.
Bruises, too, may appear,
Blemishing the darkening skin
And leaving tell-tale marks on the flesh.
In too many days, the skin will loosen its grip
Radiating the color of decay.
Slipping into sloppy sponginess.
And the scent will shift from cloying to sickening.
Overripe. And good for little.
Not even memory.

ON BEING VIRTUAL

Never here.
Nor there.
Full-time.
Not bad.
Except for lunch.
Anyone?

FEELING ANGSTY

Not dreading.
Not fearing.
Not worrying.
Not angst for real.
Just angst for what's next
When you are just not sure what is coming.
But who is?
Surety belongs to the gods.
Zeus with his thunder bolt.
Odin with his hammer.
Today surety comes in the form of blockbuster movies
Distinguished by the number in their titles.
The higher, the better.
We may not know the plot,
But we know the outcome.
Comfort in that certainty.
Angst-free.
Unlike life in all its angst.

DOUBT

A word that does not look
Like it is spelled.
D-O-U-B-T.
But when coupled with other words,
It means much.
Without a doubt.
Self-doubt.
Raising doubt.
No doubt about it.
Doubt does not look
Like it is spelled.
Only how it feels.

INSIGHT

You know you have it
When whatever people tell you
You already know.

FOCUS

He values focus.
Sharp. Keen. Practiced.
And always on himself.

QUIET QUITTING

When you feel you have done enough,
Even though your boss says he needs more.

When you feel that no one appreciates the hours you have tallied,
And the work you have done.

When you feel your bosses want perfection,
But you lack the gumption.

When others around you seem weary,
Feeling like you, lost and overwhelmed.

When you feel used up because when enough is enough,
It is time to quit.

BEING COACHED

It must be this way.
Or not.
Could it not be that way?
Or not.

Trust your gut,
They say.
No, you need to listen
To others.

Finding a path
When there is no path.
Only boulders.
Getting in—no blocking— the way.

If it is clarity you seek,
Know there is none.
Discomforting, yes.
And hurting sharply.

Not this way,
Or that.
Make it your way,
But how?

BREAKING

"Break a leg" is show-biz talk for "good luck."
"If you want to make an omelet, you need to break some eggs."
"Break bad habits" to improve yourself.
Sometimes breaking things can lead to better things.
Unless those things are made of glass.
(Or the boss's ideas!)

THE BOSS

The corridors are darkened.
Cubicles silent and empty.
The chairs up straight.
The boss scowls,
"Where is everyone?"
An aide leans in, "Home, sir."
"Wasting time, I know."
"Well, sir," the aide leans back. "Productivity's up.
"We're kicking butt."
The boss growls,
"I am the one who kicks butt,
"And I want those butts back in my seats."

FIRE 'EM

"Now, they just fire 'em," he said.
"Used to provide severance. No more.
"They just cut 'em. Kinda like pro football.
"'Cept they don't get hurt. At least on the outside.
"On the inside it's a different matter.
"Been working 10, 15 years, then out on their asses.
"That hurts. Some of them find work real fast.
"Others, not so fast.
"Regardless, they don't bounce back so easy.
"They feel left out. And they are.
"Some start drinking more. As a way of killing the pain.
"Not that they did anything to deserve it.
"And they are good workers. Some of the best.
"Yeah, it's different now.
"They just fire 'em."

SELF-KNOWLEDGE

Brilliance.
Every head turns at your words.
Shimmering.
Searing.
Soaring.
You think.

Wisdom.
A rueful smile maybe when you speak.
Sharing.
Caring.
Knowing.
They understand.
So you think.

THE LIES WE TELL OURSELVES

There is comfort in the lies we tell.
Not to others, of course.
Only to ourselves.

Within our lies we can be ourselves.
Free of expectation.
Unburdened by truth.

Such lies give shelter to our image.
They keep us who we want to be.
But are not.

Yes, we will do that thing one day.
Just not now.
Better to stay inside. Ourselves.

These are little lies, of course.
Not major. Strictly minor.
Passing fancy really.

Acting with Humility and Wisdom

Humility is a virtue, no doubt.
But gaining humility requires more than virtue.
Hard work. Sacrifice. Selflessness.
Humility demands a sublimation of ego, but not of will.
Willpower gives us the strength to step back,
So that others may go forward.
Humility enables us to see the light in others,
Rather than our reflection.

Work hard to understand yourself.
Pay attention.
Attend to what you have observed.
Do not fear your shortcomings.
Use them as your guides to move forward.
Take heart from your failures.
Gain lessons from your mistakes.
Forgive yourself so you can forgive others.
Demonstrate kindness to yourself as a means of
expressing kindness to others.
Practice, practice, practice.

Hardships often prepare ordinary people for an extraordinary destiny.
—C. S. Lewis

How We Act

Looking for ways to make the positive difference
is the challenge everyone faces.
It is easy to become discouraged when the change we seek meets resistance.
But then if it did then perhaps it would not be worth our effort.

COURAGE

Is it Bravery
Fortitude,
Resilience, or
Strength?
All of these and more.
Shaped by love for others,
Steeled by hard truths,
Courage can be a moment of heroism, or
A daily struggle to bear witness.
Courage is the commitment to persevere
In light and
In darkness.

HEART

Called the "little brain."
It does not think.
It only feels.
It does not remember.
It only senses.
It does not compute.
It only guides.
Pumping. Pumping. Pumping.
For us.

FIRE

Passion for others burns brightly.
And is extinguished in time.
Passion for the righteous burns all the time.
If we stoke the fire.

WISDOM

None of us knows everything.
Though at times we act as if we do.
Being with others tempers our mental aggrandizement
In favor of learning from others.
For the better of both.

GRACE

The spirit abides within us to do good.
Our choice is to heed the abundance
Or chose another path.
Community points in the right direction.
Making grace our given path.

HOPE

Hope is not a method, they say.
True enough!
Hope is that glimmer within that rings with possibility.
Hope is not an end
But it can be a beginning.
A place to start
Hope can also be a middle.
And a way post on the way.
Hope can be a dream unfulfilled.
Used wisely, hope provokes
Thoughts and effort.
Action and execution.
Hope fulfilled.

SOUL

Something beyond the senses.
Cognition of something else.
It is heart and mind commingled with
Life. Spirit. Soul.

PURPOSE

Overworked
Overcome
Overwrought
Overdone
Overs too many
Yet within all the overing
Might be the possibility of pulling one over
Making what seems impossible
Possible.
Then it might be not over
But something just begun.

HUMILITY

Humility is a virtue, no doubt.
But gaining humility requires more than virtue.
Hard work. Sacrifice. Selflessness.
Humility demands a sublimation of ego, but not of will.
Willpower gives us the strength to step back,
So that others may go forward.
Humility enables us to see the light in others,
Rather than our reflection.

GRATITUDE

If this is the worst that happens,
Take a deep breath.
Exhale slowly.
Remind yourself of your blessings
Take another deep breath.
Exhale slowly.
Smile in gratitude.

THINK

To think is to consider.
To ponder and to wonder.
As well as to challenge.
Thinking requires effort.
Although work is never without effort,
Forethought makes it seem so.
Thinking truly is our work as we ask:
What's been done? Or left undone?
Answers provide our next steps.
Steps that lead us to know more and do more.

SELF-AWARENESS

Work hard to understand yourself.

Pay attention.

Attend to what you have observed.

Do not fear your shortcomings.

Use them as your guides to move forward.

Take heart from your failures.

Gain lessons from your mistakes.

Forgive yourself so you can forgive others.

Demonstrate kindness to yourself as a means of expressing kindness to others.

Practice, practice, practice.

COMPASSION

When you feel what another feels,
We call it empathy.
When you act on that feeling,
We call it compassion.
From the Latin, compati,
Meaning "to suffer with."
For us English speakers, it is not we who suffer.
It is we who lessen the suffering.
We act for the benefit of others
Because we know they need us.
Without asking.

DECISIONS

Decisions made are decisions done.
Consequence is what becomes of them.
Regard decisions as written in stone,
Or as mere stepping stones?
Undo them? Or persist in them?
What we do matters as much as how we do it.
With logic, reason, and, let's hope, some heart.

KEEPING UP

What gets you up in the morning?
A good question so often ignored.
Because in the rush-rush of the day
We have so much to do
Trying hard to keep ahead of the game
Or even abreast of it.
Too often we are too busy to think
"Just get it done" becomes our mantra.
Another task.
Another hour.
Another morning.

WHEN WORDS FAIL

Words fail.
We struggle to say what's "right,"
Without knowing what right means.
So, we are left with looks and gestures.
Eye to eye.
Hand to hand.
Shoulder to shoulder.
Connection, yes.

RESILIENCE

Yes, I can.
So simple to say when things are going well.
Not so easy when…
Your project has been cancelled.
Your team has been disbanded.
Your boss—whom you like—has been transferred.
Your job has been eliminated.
So hard then when fortune turns to misfortune.
But when you realize that what happened to you,
Is not you,
Then you can decide your next move.
Slowly. Deliberately. Carefully.
Maybe not as strong as before,
But adding muscle with every move you take.

SOLITUDE

Aloneness, yes.
But not loneliness.
Solitude is a gift to self.
To reflect, dream, muse, and create.
Solitude is a connection to ourselves.
It can open the door to awareness of self.
Understanding who we are and what we can do.
For ourselves and for others.
Solitude therefore opens the door to connection with others.
An antidote to loneliness.

JOY

Joy is not a destination.
It is more a journey.
It is not one of pure happiness.
More of struggle.
Yet in the pushing-and-pulling, we find our true selves.
Open. Ready. Able.
To help others.
And in doing so.
Ourselves.

THE FOURTH LETTER IN GRACE

Candor—speaking up
Courage—standing up for others
Commitment—recognizing responsibility
Companionship—being there
Compassion—showing care to others (and yourself)
Cheerleading—a rah-rah with heart and soul
Community—holding together and believing together
All of which, if you think about it, add up to one word—
Connectedness.
What we are seeking when we are
Alone.
Together.
Or somewhere in between.

ORDINARY

Some start companies
Building organizations bold and caring.
Others climb mountains,
Both real and imagined.
We say they have purpose.
Us?
We earn for our families,
In jobs that we may like, or not.
We teach our children to care, and
Love them still when they do not.
We show up for others when we are not asked.
The mountains we climb are what we do
In our own ordinary way.

FRIENDS

Friends are friends when they stand beside and behind us.
They see us as who we are.
Imperfect, yes, but approachable, accessible, and kind.
Friends think the best of us.
And want it to be so.
When we fall short, friends remind us of our better selves.

Some of us have friends for life.
Others for only a short time.
Friendship is not measured in length of time,
But instead in the depth of commitment.

True friends are a presence that makes us better.
Friendship is not transactional.
It is transformative.
We are wiser for their presence and their love.

TRANSFORMATION

So often in movies
There is that moment when the hero
Facing impossible odds
Suddenly decides to take action.
The camera pulls back
As the music crescendos
Revealing the hero standing tall.
Hurrah!
We smile
Secretly hoping to hear that same music.

MAY THE BLESSING

Philosopher-poet John O'Donohue wrote reams of poems.
Many were blessings.
As befit his previous priestly calling.
Each line of his blessings begins with "May."
May you think free…
May you feel the ground…
May you know you are loved.
And so forth.

May is the intercession between
Mother and child.
Pastor and parish.
Leader and follower.

May is a door opener.
Invoking, it says, "Are you listening, Lord?"
Or to whomever you are addressing.

May is a kind word.
An invitation, as the French would say, to "parlez."
To have a conversation with a Higher Power "up there."
Or a "higher power" down here.

May is a good word.
One full of grace.
Smiling as I write this.
As children, we asked intercessions from
Mary, full of grace.

May we all find more mays.
May the light snuff out the dark.
May despair lose to hope.
May sorrow drown in joy.
May. May. May.

Lead with SPINE

*Leading with spine is rooted in the moral authority
we exert to act upon the "better angels of our nature."*

Strength is standing up for what you believe and acting on those beliefs. "Moral authority," wrote Stephen Covey, "comes from following universal and timeless principles like honesty, integrity, treating people with respect."

Principle is rooted in purpose. It becomes the very marrow of the spine, giving it the ability to remain upright in the face of adversity.

Integrity is the expression of ethical behavior. Telling the truth and being accountable is fundamental to behaving with honor, living not just for oneself but for the good of others.

Nurture is the caring side of leadership. It means investing yourself in the development of others. Coaching is a form of nurturing, finding ways to guide while challenging others to do their best.

Energy is necessary to catalyze the organization. Leaders need to invest—and exert—themselves in creating opportunities for others.

It is not by muscle, speed, or physical dexterity that great things are
achieved, but by reflection, force of character, and judgment.
—Cicero

Stories to Inspire

Often the best way to seek positive change
is to look at what has come before us.
Look to those who have made the world better for others.
Their example reveals what is possible if we make the effort to do our best.

SALLY HELGESEN—GIVING WOMEN VOICE TO LEAD

The first time I spoke with Sally Helgesen was on an airplane flying from San Diego to Detroit. We had both attended a conference where I was first introduced to Marshall Goldsmith (more about him later in this chapter). Marshall had lavishly praised Sally's work. And rightly so. Sally is from my home state of Michigan, and we have stayed in touch. I have learned much from her and her work, and I have found her to be a tremendous supporter of mine.

Sally has been writing about women's leadership roles since the 1980s. Her best-known book is *How Women Rise*, which she coauthored with Marshall. She followed it with another book, *Rising Together: How We Can Bridge Divides and Create a More Inclusive Workplace*. It brings her thinking about diversity, inclusion, and equity into sharp focus, illuminating a path forward she calls a "culture of belonging."

According to Sally, a culture of belonging is achieved when a majority of people "feel ownership in the organization, believe they are valued for their potential as well as their contributions, [and] perceive that how they matter is not strictly tied to their positional powers."

IDENTIFYING TRIGGERS

A grand statement, yes. So how do we achieve it?

The short answer is to change behaviors. When we become aware of how we are acting in the presence of others, Sally writes, we can identify what we need to do differently. As she told me in an interview, look for triggers (obstacles) that get in the way of us being our best around others. Such triggers include a lack of visibility, a lack of confidence, misperceptions, and poor use of humor.[1]

One trigger is unconscious bias. It is human nature to trust what we know and distrust what we don't. Calling it out is appropriate, but we often focus on what separates us rather than what unites us. "It alienates us from one another… We're constantly thinking, 'Oh, well, this person's background might be different,' and a sense of unease sets in."

Worse, individuals who differ from the group on the basis of gender or ethnicity feel marginalized. "They feel stereotyped. They feel unheard. They feel under-recognized for their individuality. It's not a good thing."

Marginalization can occur even with good intentions. Sally tells the story of a younger client she was working with who had been invited to attend a corporate strategy session. It was senior management's way of acting inclusively. As a more junior executive, the young woman was excited, only to learn that she and her colleagues had been placed at the back of the room. Her client told Sally, "In order to say anything, I had to make my boss's boss turn around to hear me."

TAKEAWAY LESSONS
The final chapter is a kind of handbook titled *Formal Enlistment* that outlines how to put the *Rising Together* principles into practice. "It's the informal engagement where you're asking people to give you feedback on how you're doing. You're disclosing what you're doing in a spirit of honesty, and you're getting others to share their feedback. It's a great way to build relationships."

Reflecting on her work in the past, Sally says, "Women are in a lot better place than they were when I started working in women's leadership thirty years ago." Building an inclusive workplace for all will require "positive culture change that will benefit a broad range of people who may be under-recognized or undervalued in the workplace now."

[1] *Sally Helgesen: Grace Under Pressure podcast https://youtu.be/S5dU-D0EPHI*
Sally Helgesen Rising Together: How We Can Bridge Divides and Create a More Inclusive Workplace Balance 2023

GARRY RIDGE—CREATING THE LEARNING CULTURE

I first saw Garry Ridge at a 100 Coaches meeting in January 2020. We did not meet face-to-face. COVID struck, and it would be a couple of years before we connected again—this time at The Purpose Summit, organized by our mutual colleague and friend, Davin Salvagno. We have stayed in closer touch since, and I am indebted to Garry for the support he has shown me.

Garry Ridge, CEO Emeritus of WD-40 Company, practiced this lesson firsthand. At the start of the Great Recession in 2008, as Garry traveled from office to office and country to country, people would ask him how he was doing. At first, he thought people were asking about his welfare and how he was holding up. Later, it dawned on him that people were really asking, "How are we doing?" They were looking to Garry for answers, clarity, and hope amid a crisis.

A native of Australia, Garry has the bearing of a no-nonsense guy who loves nonsense. That is, Garry is down-to-earth, fun-loving, and passionate about helping people do their best to achieve for themselves and for the company. His fundamentals are people, purpose, strategy, execution, and freedom. People know their jobs, learn from them, enable others to plan and execute, and have the space to experiment.

In an interview for my LinkedIn Live show *Grace Under Pressure*, Garry shared his philosophy on leadership and what it takes to lead in times of crisis.[2]

ON WORKING

Imagine a place where you go to work every day; you make a contribution to something bigger than yourself. You learn something new, you're protected and set free by a compelling set of values. And you go home happy. Our job as leaders is to create that place because happy people make happy families, happy families create happy communities, and happy communities create a happy world. And my gosh, we need a happy world.

---

[2] *Garry Ridge: Grace Under Pressure podcast https://youtu.be/5OvvQNV2Jes*

On the "soul-sucking CEO"
(A puppet character Garry uses to make his points)

He's the master of control. He's the know-it-all. He's corporate royalty. He's spent a lot of time fighting his way up the corporate royalty channel. He thinks learning is for losers because he has all the answers. Most particularly, his ego eats his empathy instead of his empathy eating his ego. He must always be right. He loves fear-based culture. Micro-management is essential, followed through when it comes to what he does. And he hates feedback.

On hope
You must have hope. Being hopeless means you're not going to deliver on what you would need to do. Hope is about having pragmatic optimism. You've got to be pragmatic and optimistic at the same time. One key attribute of a servant leader is being a champion of hope.

On the gift of belonging
The gift of belonging is remembering that one of the most significant needs we have is the gift of actually belonging. And, you know, we talk about our tribe in a way that it's a group of people that come together to both protect and feed each other.

On teaching leadership
I think the greatest way to learn is to teach. And I'm so grateful that, for the last twelve or so years, I've been able to gather with cohorts of people to examine and discuss some of the principles of leadership we have. And you know, one of the advantages I have in teaching their program is that I'm not an academic; I'm a practitioner. So being able to share my scar tissue has been a benefit.

Note: Two years after our interview, Garry (with Martha Finney) amplified these thoughts in his book *Any Dumbass Can Do It: Learning Moments from an Everyday CEO of a Multi-Billion Company*.[3]

[3] *Garry Ridge and Martha Finney Any Dumbass Can Do It: Learning Moments from an Everyday CEO of a Multi-Billion Company Matt Holt Books 2025*

ANNE CHOW—THINKING AND ACTING BIGGER

Anne Chow was a guest on my podcast *Grace Under Pressure*. She was there to promote her new book Lead Bigger. Our conversation was anything but promotional. Anne was warm, friendly, and wholly engaged. It was evident that, as former CEO of AT&T Business—and the first woman and woman of color to hold that title—she had made her mark not for her business acumen, but for her ability to connect with individuals, making each feel special.

"Leading small is almost literally not having a broad perspective, not thinking about the consequences of what you're doing," Anne told me in an interview. It's "being incredibly transactional in your nature, and quite frankly being very self-oriented, perhaps not intentionally, but being very self-oriented as opposed to being selfless, in a way." [4]

Anne advocates that to truly lead bigger, you need to "widen your perspective to have greater performance and impact." This concept is not new to Anne. What struck me was that we are always told to think bigger, especially if we're in a rut, if there's a disruption that's happened in the marketplace, a new technology, a challenge in the workforce, a challenge on a geopolitical basis, think bigger since we were young, since we were little kids."

Doing this requires the power of purpose to focus on work that matters with engaged employees who can innovate and adapt to change. "It takes people to drive a business; it takes people to be the heart and soul of the business. The business does not drive people. And the quicker you realize that, the quicker you realize that it is our job as leaders. Leadership is all about people. You manage things, you lead people," says Anne.

---

[4] *Anne Chow: Grace Under Pressure podcast https://youtu.be/zMczOtC_3Qs*

Doing so can create a sense of community, whether it's within your organization among employees or with your customers and stakeholders. As Anne says, "It's ultimately about people. So that sense of community, that sense of connection is vital in order for you to get done what you need to get done in the most effective and efficient ways."

The subtitle of Anne's book is *The Transformative Power of Inclusion*. In other words, to lead bigger, you need to think beyond your own experiences and horizons. This engagement can only occur when you involve people from all different backgrounds. Involvement means inclusion, welcoming them to contribute and to create a community.[5]

Presence is essential to the notion of inclusion. But it would help if you were smart about what you are asking for, says Anne. "And it's up to us as leaders to really understand what productivity really is, and what it is that we need. I don't think there's a single person who would disagree that in person is better for building deep connection, but it is not necessary to get every bit of every job done."

[5] *Anne Chow Lead Bigger: The Transformative Power of Inclusion New York: Simon & Schuster 2024*

ALAN MULALLY—CEO FOR OUR TIMES

When Alan Mulally was selected as CEO of the Ford Motor Company in 2006,
the once-vaunted automaker was facing severe financial difficulties. As one who
had worked for Ford, first as a speechwriter and later as an executive coach,
I sent him a copy of my latest book. To my surprise, a week later, I received a
handwritten thank-you note, complete with Alan's signature icon—a hand-
drawn airliner.

We kept in touch over the years and met at a Ford dealer meeting. By then,
Ford was on the rebound and had made significant progress. Alan, in short,
was a rock star to dealers; everyone wanted to have their picture taken with
him. Alan obliged. I watched him pose with over seven hundred dealers in one
evening. He did not do the grip-and-grin. No, he greeted each one personally
and asked about their business. He even helped pose groups for pictures,
including ones with the young staffers who were arranging the photo sessions.
And get this: Alan posed for the picture for four consecutive nights. Could
he have been doing something else? Of course. But Alan knew it was his
responsibility to be with his customers. And they loved him for it.

Business Plan Review

When he first came to Ford, Alan faced reality by getting his team to focus on
the issues and commit to fixing them. One way he did this was by convening
weekly meetings with his direct reports (Business Plan Reviews), where heads
of various functions reported on the status of their projects. Attendees used
color codes: green (all good), yellow (having difficulties), or red (in trouble).
At first, the executives—afraid of getting themselves on the wrong side of their
new boss—reported all green.

Once they understood that Alan was not out for scalps, they realized that accurate reporting was necessary for the company's survival. Alan also insisted that the executives collaborate across functions and work together to solve problems.

The process worked, and Ford was restored to fiscal health. In time, Fortune magazine named Alan the third-best executive in the world—right behind Pope Francis. Since he retired from Ford in 2014, he has been teaching organizations how to bring people together for a common cause to achieve agreed-upon goals.

One of Alan's core beliefs is the concept of love, a value he learned from his mother, who preached it and embodied it for her son and her family. It was further nurtured by Frances Hesselbein, a former CEO of the Girl Scouts, with whom Alan became well acquainted. Frances believed that "to serve is to live."

Alan's philosophy of "Working Together" aligns with the concept that "life's work of service is our love made visible." This sense of service extends beyond professional duties, encompassing how we interact within our community and with our family and ourselves. Such a connection opens the door to learning more or leaning on the spiritual side of life.

ALAINA LOVE—THE HEALER

Alaina Love is a healer. And that has been evident from when I first met her sometime in the late 2010s. I knew her work from the column she wrote for *Businessweek* (now *Bloomberg Businessweek*), for which I was also contributing. We arranged to meet in Washington, D.C., and immediately hit it off. Over the years, I have counted on Alaina's wise counsel in coaching and in my writing. It was she who gave me the structure for my first outing in poetry, *Grace Notes: Leading in an Upside-Down World*.

And so, with great anticipation, I came to know her book, *Permission to Be You: Discover Your Purpose and Passions to Bring Your Best Self to Everything—and Everyone*. Alaina's expertise is in helping others heal by discovering meaning and purpose. In her new book, *Love,* she reveals her journey to healing and purpose and, in the process, provides readers with a guide to their journey.[6]

For Alaina, purpose is the starting point, but it only works when you add passion—what you like and want to do. When purpose and passion are aligned, individuals learn more about who they are and how they fit into the larger world.

Passion is rooted in your value system. As Alaina writes, "In essence, your values define how you will show up in times of ease and times of challenge, allowing you to apply your passions to navigate situations as your best self."

Alaina's book is based on decades of research she has conducted into these topics. One result is the Passion Profiler, an assessment that individuals and companies use in professional development efforts. The book also integrates key attributes and definitions of personality styles (archetypes).

---

[6] *Alaina Love Permission to Be You: Discover Your Purpose and Passions to Bring Your Best Self to Everything— and Everyone Vancouver, British Columbia: Page Two 2025*

Career choices

While much of the book focuses on self-development, it offers key insights into defining one's career. Alaina posits the "evolutionary mindset." "Careers are not fixed pathways; they are transformative experiences. As you develop deeper self-knowledge, grow capabilities, and progress through different roles, your career will evolve as your passion mastery grows, and how you manage all this will evolve with you."

In other words, as you grow and develop individually and professionally, you may want to pursue new opportunities as well as new careers. Toward this end, this chapter provides self-assessments and questions to help an individual identify their personal drivers and apply them accordingly.

Giving yourself permission

In conclusion, the book is a handbook-like section that distills the essence of Alaina's teachings. Called "Ten Permissions to Give Yourself," it focuses on life's challenges and the shortcomings we face. The first is "Permission to Receive Love," followed by "Permission to Fail." These two obstacles address the notion that we are not worthy and, therefore, unable to accomplish our goals. Nonsense, argues Alaina. Each of us has the capacity to give as well as to receive. By identifying such negative thoughts, Alaina gives us the permission we need to give ourselves.

Alaina concludes her book with this exhortation.
"Wrest the megaphone of opinions and perspectives from the hands of people who are not living your life, and begin listening to your intuition. You can be confident that it will guide you correctly. Yes, you are where you've come from. But you can also decide to live the life you want to create. Permit yourself to start now. "

MARSHALL GOLDSMITH—EARNING YOUR LIFE

It was in La Jolla at a seaside hotel in the early 2000s when I first met Marshall Goldsmith. I vividly recall seeing Marshall strolling down the boardwalk, smiling at everyone he encountered, and greeting me for the first time with a firm handshake and, of course, a broad smile. Since that time, I have been in his orbit, most recently as a member of 100 Coaches, which he founded. This organization is comprised of executive coaches, business executives, and talented folks from academia and science.

Marshall is a legend in human development because he is one of the seminal figures who pioneered the potential of executive coaching. Coaching over three-hundred CEOs gave him an unmatched cache.

His impact, however, emanates not from his credentials. Instead, it is his plain-spoken "street cred." In-person, as in print, Marshall is a generous soul. He makes the complex simple, but not by giving you the answers. Instead, he challenges you to think for yourself. One of his founding practices, shared for decades, is feedforward. As Marshall says, "Feedback comprises people's opinions of your past behavior. Feedforward represents other people's ideas that you should be using in the future."

This approach forms the basis of Stakeholder-Centered Coaching, a process that enables leaders to learn from stakeholders who have a vested interest in their success. The process requires vulnerability, but the payoff is two-fold.

THE EARNED LIFE

In his book *The Earned Life: Lose Regret, Choose Fulfillment*, written with Mark Reiter, he describes a trap that so many of us fall into: the Great Western Disease. He frames it with the words "I'll be happy when…" [7]

Nothing wrong with aspirations, but to let them define you, or worse, deprive you of joy on the way up, is heartbreaking. Marshall urges a different path, which he calls "flip the script."

Step one: "Do for yourself what you have done for others." You have shared advice with others when they could not see it for themselves. Therefore, "you are capable of imagining a new path. You've done it for others. Do it for yourself."

Step two: Ask yourself, "What do you want to do for the rest of your life?"

Marshall offers the "Earning Checklist," anchored in four attributes he wrote about in his doctoral thesis when he was 27 years old: motivation, ability, understanding, and confidence. Delving more deeply, Marshall dissects each in ways that challenge the reader to think about why they are motivated, what capabilities they possess, and how our understandings have shaped us. Confidence is critical. As Marshall writes, "confidence is the product of all your other positive virtues and choices, and then it returns the favor by making you even stronger in those areas."

NOTHING HAPPENS OVERNIGHT

"Earning your life is the long game. Check that: It's the long game." Playing that game requires two things: "self-awareness and situation-awareness." Work these disciplines until you feel that your earned life becomes a habit, something you do as part of your routine. In short, such a habit enables you to become a more fulfilled version of yourself. [8]

Note of caution. Credibility is not a "do it once" endeavor. "It's one thing to be competent, it's another thing to gain credibility with one but not the other," Marshall writes. "You have to earn it twice." Failure to reinforce your credibility diminishes your ability to "make a positive difference—and lessens the impact of your life."

As Marshall says, "Leaders earned their employee's respect. Employees earned their CEO's gratitude."

The Earned Life explores what life can offer us if we are willing to shirk self-imposed constraints. If we are ready to invest ourselves in becoming our better selves—however we define it—then, and only then, can we say that we have deserved our place. We have earned it.

After nearly fifty years of exploring human behavior, *The Earned Life* offers insights into what makes us tick and how we can tick over even better.

---

[7] *Marshall Goldsmith and Mark Reiter. The Earned Life: Lose Regret, Choose Fulfillment New York: Crown Currency 2022*

[8] *Marshall Goldsmith and Mark Reiter. The Earned Life: Lose Regret, Choose Fulfillment New York: Crown Currency 2022*

HARRY KRAEMER, JR.—LIVING FOR A GREATER CAUSE

The first time I met Harry Kraemer was in an elevator on the way down. Harry was on his way to the gym and wearing a Kellogg School of Management t-shirt. My wife, herself a Kellogg alumna, was with me, and I introduced myself. That began a connection that has blossomed over the years. Harry has been an inspiration to me.

When Harry stepped down as CEO of Baxter, Inc., he was unsure what he would do next. Dean Don Jacobs of the Kellogg School of Management knew precisely what he wanted Harry to do—teach.

In 2006, Andrew Youn, a fellow Kellogg alumnus, decided to use his MBA to help the farmers of Kenya increase their crop yields. After meeting Andrew at his fifth class reunion in 2011, Harry partnered with Andrew to create The One Acre Fund to assist the farmers in Kenya. The Fund now helps farmers in a total of nine countries in sub-Saharan Africa, including Rwanda, Uganda, and Tanzania.

What Harry has done—as he documents in his newest book *Your Values-Based Legacy: Making a Difference at Every Phase of Life*—is to make his life's work his legacy. As Harry illustrates, legacy is not just what you do upon retirement; it is the sum of contributions you make throughout your life.[9]

Values are the principles you hold dear. As Harry has said, values are not preferences; they are principles. Identifying them comes from many sources, but a critical one for Harry is self-reflection, something he practices daily with simple questions about what he did that day and how he might do better the next.

Harry writes in his new book, "For years, in my classes at Kellogg about becoming a values-based leader, I've asked students who they expect will deal with all these problems (poverty, hunger, injustice, etc.)." Students' responses indicate that someone else will. "And everybody refers to these people by the same name: 'those guys,' a gender-neutral term for people with money, power and influence."

Harry's response to his students and the audiences to whom he speaks is simple: "Guess what? We are those guys!" The problems facing the world do not belong to someone else; they belong to us, because what harms some of us harms all of us—maybe not directly, but indirectly through affecting global stability, the climate crisis, and government spending.

[9] *Harry M. Jansen Kraemer, Jr. Values-Based Legacy: Making a Difference at Every Phase and Phase of Life Hoboken, New Jersey: Wiley 2025*

JEAN RENOIR—A PERSON HERO

There is a painting that hangs in the Musee d'Orange in Paris of Jean Renoir as a young child. It was painted by his father, Auguste Renoir, one of the giants of the Impressionist school.

Jean served as a cavalryman in World War I and was wounded. He later served as a reconnaissance pilot. After the war, Jean became a film director, helming some of the great films of his era, most notably *Rules of the Game* and *La Grand Illusion*.

When I was in college in the early seventies, I did a photo series reminiscent of Jean's comic film *A Day in the Country*.

I sent them to Mr. Renoir, then living in Beverly Hills. His wife, Dido, wrote me a nice thank-you note saying that Jean liked what I had done.

Merci, Mr. Renoir.

PHARMACIST WHO CARES

It was my second visit to the pharmacy. Patients were coming in to pick up prescriptions and get their COVID-19 or flu vaccinations. It was busy, and during my two visits over the past two weeks, I had noticed that some patients had issues related to insurance hiccups or unfilled scripts.

At the center of the activity was a tall man in his sixties, the head pharmacist. The younger pharmacists and technicians repeatedly came to him for instruction and clarification. In some instances, he went directly to the patient or called the physician's office on the patient's behalf. He also dispensed medications and administered vaccinations.

And he did it all with a smile, one that was unfailing, radiating warmth and care in situations where some patients were feeling the stress of not knowing whether their scripts would be filled. He never flinched. He treated everyone—old and young—with courtesy. And he spoke more gently and slowly for those older than himself.

As I left for the second time, I walked to his consultation window and complimented him on his relentless patience and kindness. Before I could finish speaking, he said, "It's them. My staff," as he gestured to the young folks around him. "They do the work."

I laughed and said he was demonstrating what authentic leadership is all about—focusing on serving others and recognizing the efforts of those who make it happen.

FRANCES HESSELBEIN: TO SERVE IS TO LIVE

Frances Hesselbein exuded warmth and compassion. I sensed that from her the first time we spoke. I was profiling her for one of my books, and she graciously made time for me. Later, I met her at the Four Seasons restaurant in New York City at a book party for Marshall Goldsmith, one of her proteges. Again, the warmth and kindness made me, a virtual stranger, feel right at home. It is little wonder that her friend Peter Drucker hailed her when she led the Girl Scouts of America as the greatest CEO he had ever met.

LIFE LESSON

"To serve is to live," she taught us.
We listened.
And wondered how.
So,
She showed by example how to
Listen with an open heart
Stand tall for what's right
Understand differences
Seek common cause
Be grateful
Find joy in work and play
In short,
To love.

In memory of Frances Hesselbein (1915-2022)

MARK GOULSTON: A GOOD MAN REMEMBERED

Mark Goulston M.D. was a man who made his presence felt by connecting so well and so deeply with people he thought he ought to know better. Fortunately, I was one of his chosen, and we maintained a steady connection for nearly 20 years until his passing at 75. A psychiatrist turned executive coach, Mark could size up an issue with almost spontaneous clarity. It was a gift that he shared with nearly everyone he met, and nearly everyone who met him feels a special connection with him. That was the kind of human—kind, compassionate, and warm—Mark was.

For Mark

Let me put it this way…
He would say.
And in an instant,
He would have you back on your heels.
In wonder.
How could he know that about me?
For decades, I have known his voice.
In print. On video. In person.
And I quoted him. Often.
In print. On video. In person.
I knew for years he was ill.
He told me so.
Not with rancor, nor bitterness, nor even regret.
He lived as he wrote, spoke and shared.
The purpose of life, he said, is to serve others.
A mensch in his tradition.
A wise man and a kind man
In all traditions.

In memory of Mark Goulston, MD (1947-2022)

Creating a Culture of Service

**How can you develop a mindset of
service to your colleagues?**

Listen, don't judge
(Keep an open mind)

Replace "have to" with "want to"
(When it comes to doing your work)

Promote benefits over activity
(How does this help others?)

Adopt a me-last attitude
(Be humble)

Share credit and take blame
(Step out of the limelight)

*"The greatest untapped source of motivation
is a sense of service to others."*

POPE FRANCIS—PASTOR

Pastor.
That is what he saw himself as.
And how he wanted the world to see him.
Not as regal, not as exalted, but as a shepherd
Tending souls, not sheep.
Souls who wanted counsel and guidance.
Not sheep who would sit in silence.
He was a shepherd who would seek out those
Whom so many shunned.
Because they were different and
"Not like us."
Understanding was his hallmark,
Mercy was his trademark.
He was one who ate in a dining hall
Stood in line to get his own meals.
Sitting with others, not apart from them.
Sharing. Joking. Laughing.
His name was Francis.
Like the man from Assisi.

ROBERT REDFORD—USING THE POWER OF FAME FOR GOOD

Robert Redford once said that if you were a movie star, few would take you seriously. While that may have been the norm for some, it did not apply to him.

Redford was a superstar, the kind Hollywood used to have but is less common today. He had been a screen presence for sixty years, starring in such memorable classics as *Butch Cassidy and the Sundance Kid* (with fellow icon Paul Newman) and *The Sting* (again with Newman). There were also hits like *All the President's Men*, *Three Days of the Condor*, and *Out of Africa*.

Redford applied his talents behind the camera, serving as director on *Ordinary People* (for which he won an Oscar) and later directing eight other films, including *A River Runs Through It*, *Quiz Show*, and *The Horse Whisperer*.

Movies were not his only passion. Believing firmly in filmmaking as an art form, he launched the Sundance Film Festival in his adopted home state of Utah. This festival launched landmark films by many who would go on to become major directors, including Quentin Tarantino and Ava DuVernay.

Living as he did in Utah, experiencing nature was paramount, and so he became an ardent environmentalist, using his public platform to raise awareness of conservation and the preservation of natural wilderness.

FACING ADVERSITY

Idyllic, yes, but not always. Redford lost a daughter in infancy; a son, age 58, died of cancer; his daughter experienced a near-death auto accident; and his first marriage ended in divorce. Later, he suffered financial losses and had to sell his stake in Sundance.[10]

In fact, his early life gave no hint of his future. His mother died when he was a teenager and that loss set him somewhat adrift. He earned a baseball scholarship to the University of Colorado but dropped out in part because he preferred partying to studying. He went to Europe for a year and made a living by selling street drawings. He had a knack for illustration.

What Redford reminds us is to reflect on what we have accomplished by focusing on what we have done, rather than what we might have done. Take pride in your accomplishments, but do not dwell on them. Continue to pursue new horizons in your life and career.

Bob Woodward, legendary reporter for the *Washington Post* and who was portrayed by Redford in *All the President's Men*, said, "I loved him, and admired him—for his friendship, his fiery independence, and the way he used any platform he had to help make the world better, fairer, brighter for others."[11]

---

[10] Brooks Barnes "Robert Redford, Screen Idol Turned Director and Activist, Dies at 89" *New York Times* September 16, 2025 https://www.nytimes.com/2025/09/16/movies/robert-redford-dead.html

[11] Benjamin Mullin "Bob Woodward Remembers Robert Redford" *New York Times* September 16, 2025 https://www.nytimes.com/2025/09/16/business/media/bob-woodward-robert-redford.html

JAMES LOVELL—PERSISTENCE IN THE FACE OF ADVERSITY

James Lovell, the commander of Apollo 13, which suffered an oxygen tank leak two-hundred miles from Earth, almost never had the opportunity to fly that mission.

As NPR reporter Russell Lewis noted in his remembrance of Lovell's passing, perseverance was his extraordinary strength. Lovell did not get into the United States Naval Academy on his first try. He was later accepted, became a combat fighter pilot, and qualified for the test pilot program at Edwards Air Force Base. He did not qualify for the Mercury astronaut program, but was later accepted into the Gemini program. Again, a second try was successful.

These setbacks steeled Lovell to become an astronaut who could handle the pressures in times of adversity. Fear was not an option in times of crisis. As Lovell told the *New York Times* years later, "We were all test pilots, and the only thing we could do was try to get home," he said in the 1995 article. "The idea of despair never occurred to us because we were always optimistic we would get home." [12]

It was this kind of bravery that transfixed the nation, and decades later—after Lovell published his story of the mission—led to a landmark motion picture directed by Ron Howard and starring Tom Hanks as Lovell.

One thing Lovell noted about the Apollo 13 mission was NASA's leadership. It scrambled together ad hoc solutions to engineer fixes that could make the command module safe enough to return to Earth.

As Lovell told NPR in 2014, what Apollo 13 demonstrated was "what you could do with good leadership in an organization—good leadership fosters teamwork, and teamwork and initiative, when you faced a problem, used initiative or imagination to try to solve the problem, because everything doesn't flow freely in life and things change." [13]

Perseverance is something that strengthens as we use it. Learning from Lovell's example, we do not give up immediately when we face obstacles. Resilience emerges, as it did for Lovell, from setbacks. Sometimes achievements come easily, but those that require extra effort are the ones that prepare us to face emerging challenges.

Although Lovell captained Apollo 8, the first mission to leave Earth's orbit and circle the Moon, he never achieved his dream of landing on the Moon. Life does not always work out as planned, but Lovell made his mark in history by turning disaster into a life-saving mission.

[12] *"James A. Lovell, Jr., Commander of Apollo 13, Is Dead at 97" New York Times https://www.nytimes.com/2025/08/08/science/space/james-a-lovell-jr-dead.html.*

[13] *Russell Lewis "Famed NASA astronaut and Apollo 13 commander Jim Lovell has died at age 97" NPR 8.08.2025 https://www.npr.org/2025/08/08/510627992/famed-nasa-astronaut-and-apollo-13-commander-jim-lovell-has-died-at-age-97*

THEOPHRASTUS—WISDOM FROM AN ANCIENT

Theophrastus, a philosopher who lived in the fourth century BC, was a prolific author of poetry, plays, and philosophy. His book *Characters* illuminates the factors that plague not only leaders, but the whole human race.[14] He writes of foibles and behaviors that get us into trouble, if we do not exercise "better angels," as President Abraham Lincoln counseled in his first inaugural address.

BEHAVIORS TO AVOID

Let's focus on a handful of the twenty-eight character flaws Theophrastus explores.

Dissimulation is "the artful disguise of words and actions, which proceeds from a bad intention." Deceit lies at the heart of dissimulation. Such behavior erodes trust, the foundation of good relations with others.

Flattery is the practice of using "words and actions… to catch men by their weak side, and so to ingratiate himself into their favor." Today, we call such behavior "sucking up," and when we see it in action, particularly at work, we find it obnoxious, especially if the flatterer seems to have the boss's ear.

Clownishness is "a want of knowledge in good breeding and common decency." Bad manners, putting self before others, and ignoring courtesies puts one at odds with others.

Theophrastus Character Edited by J. Robertson; translated by Henry Gally Independently published 2023

---

[14] *Joseph Epstein "The Ancient Greek Who Profiled Trump" Wall Street Journal 10.23.2025*

https://www.wsj.com/opinion/the-ancient-greek-who-profiled-trump-fabfb3be

Nastiness is "such a neglect of a man's person as makes him offensive to others." Such behavior makes it challenging to work with or even be in the company of such nasties.

Pride is "a contempt of everybody besides oneself." We all know pride to be self-destructive, but all too often the proud person is also consumed by hubris and cannot see past his own ego.

Cowardice is "a dejection of mind, proceeds from a fear of danger." Cowardice is the absence of bravery. While it is easy to denigrate those we deem cowardly, introspection reveals that we may all suffer from these traits, especially when the stakes are high.

Behaviors to emulate

Most of us can find traces of many of the negative behaviors mentioned above within ourselves. Acknowledging such deficits is how we begin to overcome them.

Knowing yourself is essential to leading yourself. Such self-knowledge focuses the mind on the behaviors we need to become the best version of ourselves. Accurate self-awareness is cognizant of our shortcomings and the means we need to employ to keep ourselves on the right path.

FRANKLIN ROOSEVELT—STANDING TALL WHILE SEATED

Through the haze of history, we assume that Franklin Roosevelt, the only president to serve more than two terms, breezed into the White House in the election of 1932. Nothing could be further from the truth, not that Franklin, as a young man, did not think such a thing was impossible. He modeled his career after his fifth cousin, Theodore, who was also the beloved uncle of his wife, Eleanor.

What interrupted his path was being stricken by polio in 1921. The disease rendered him unable to walk for the remainder of his life. Historian Jonathan Darman argues in his new book *Becoming FDR: The Personal Crisis that Made a President* that polio changed his outlook forever. It happened in two ways. First, it made him sympathetic to the underprivileged, particularly fellow polio sufferers. Two, it fueled the dictum Franklin's father had taught him: "Help all who are suffering. Man is dear to man." This notion challenged FDR to focus on what the government could do for the people. As a result, the patrician became a populist.[15]

Elected governor of New York in 1928, Roosevelt did not keep himself locked in Albany; he roamed the backwater byways on inspection tours of state-run facilities. He would go from facility to facility, meeting with administrators. While they met with him, Eleanor would conduct the physical inspections. She was peering into kitchens, clinics, and dormitories to see whether the administrators' reports were accurate. Eleanor became Franklin's legs since he primarily used a wheelchair. (Roosevelt did manage a kind of upright "walk" with his heavy leg braces, but the effort was never unaided and always exhausting.)

We learn that Franklin's heart was opened by the suffering he had endured, and he was determined to do what he could to improve the lives of many others. The lesson for managers is that people need to see you out and about. Roosevelt did not let his disability weaken his ability to meet and mingle with others. He was driven around in an open-top vehicle where people could see him, hear him, and, after his speeches, come and speak to him. He listened.

Darman notes that Roosevelt regarded himself as flexible. He quotes Roosevelt as saying, prior to being sworn in as president and as the Great Depression was worsening, "Let's concentrate on one thing. Save the people and the nation, and if we have to change our minds twice every day to accomplish that end, we should do it."

Roosevelt used his bon vivant air to encourage people to speak up and share their truths with him. Knowing where the boss stands may not be desirable, but for a president pushed and pulled in multiple directions, a measure of ambiguity may be acceptable. It can indicate that you are open to differing ideas before making a final decision.

Adversity reveals character. Management requires attention to detail. Leadership demands a focus on what is possible. FDR was able to do both well.

[15] Jonathan Darman *Becoming FDR: The Personal Crisis That Made a President* New York: Random House 2022

THOMAS MOSHER—CULTURE CRAFTSMAN

You can tell an organization's culture just by walking the halls —or, in this case, the factory floor.

When people you see make eye contact, smile, and say hello, you know this is a place that values human connection. And so it is with the Thomas Mosher Company, a family-owned furniture maker headquartered in Auburn, Maine.

Thomas Mosher furniture is simple in nature, inspired by both Shaker and Japanese Edo simplicity. There is a fluidity to the wood they shape and assemble by hand with wooden pegs—old-school simplicity. Timeless craftsmanship.

Thomas Mosher said, "It takes a hundred years to grow a cherry tree. The furniture made from it should last at least as long."

Thomas Mosher died in 2025. But the company he founded more than half a century ago is still going strong, continuing his legacy of craftsmanship rooted in simplicity and human dignity.

JIMMY CARTER—HUMBLE SERVANT

"Jimmy Carter Lauded for His Humility and Service," stated the *Associated Press* headline over a story about the thirty-ninths president's funeral at the National Cathedral in Washington, D.C.[16]

It is rare that we remember national leaders for their humility.

After all, you cannot be elected to high office if you lack a strong ego. President Carter certainly believed in his own abilities, and at times, he brooked little dissent and had a tendency to micro-manage.

But taken as a whole, Carter lived a life of service, and as an evangelical Christian, he sought to live by a creed that reminded believers of the need to be humble.

At his funeral, his grandsons noted Carter's commitment to service. Joshua Carter said, "He built houses for people who needed homes. He eliminated diseases in forgotten places. He waged peace anywhere in the world, wherever he saw a chance. He loved people."

Mentioning his grandmother Roslyn and their frugality, Jason Carter noted, "They were small-town people who never forgot who they were and where they were from no matter what happened in their lives."

The Carter Center, which Jason chairs, is a testament to the late president's commitment to service.

---

[16] *Bill Barrow and Chris Megerian "Jimmy Carter lauded for humility and service in Washington before being laid to rest in Georgia" Associated Press January 9, 2025 https://apnews.com/article/jimmy-carter-state-funeral-joe-biden-donald-trump-df391a578d6b4627ad500f5df03ac1ff*

LINCOLN—THE HUMORIST

The best statesman storyteller was Abraham Lincoln.

Having been a circuit-riding lawyer, he was a master at spinning yarns and not shy about poking a bit of fun at himself, including about his homely looks.[17]

One day, Lincoln was riding in the woods when he came across a mean-looking man with a gun who yelled, "Halt!" When Lincoln asked why he was being detained, the man said, "I vowed if I ever met a man uglier than myself I would shoot him on the spot." Abe replied, "If I am uglier than you, shoot away!"

Lincoln was so comfortable in his skin that when Stephen Douglas called him "two-faced" in one of their debates, Lincoln replied, "If I had another face, do you think I would wear this one?"

HUMOR IS A GREAT LEVELER.
It reveals the humanity of ourselves—the best of ourselves and the not-so-best parts. And it's the latter that brings out real character.

A leader who cannot laugh at themselves lacks self-awareness.

---

[17] *"Lincoln's Homely Looks" History Net https://www.historynet.com/lincoln-the-homely/*

WINSTON CHURCHILL—SHOWING GRACE

There is a story I have told a few times.

It involves Winston Churchill as England's Prime Minister in 1941. Churchill, who at times could be very brusque and unchivalrous, met James Allan Ward, a New Zealand airman who had risked his life as he climbed out of his Wellington bomber to extinguish a fire in one of the engines. Ward's bravery earned him the Victoria Cross, Britain's highest award for valor. [18]

His bravery, however, did not shield him from a bad case of nerves as the Prime Minister approached him. "You must feel very humble and awkward in my presence." Ward said, "Yes, sir."

Churchill, a combat vet, responded warmly, "Then you can imagine how humble and awkward I feel in yours."

[18] *James Allan Ward's story is based on research contained in https://www.perplexity.ai/search/tell-the-story-of-meeting-the-j9s3pqDUSGisd13ffta4Tw.*

Focus on Better

What can you do to make a positive difference?
Be a better friend, relative or colleague.

Find ways to compliment rather than criticize.
Affirm others' value when you critique.
Disagree over issues, not people.
Call on your "better angels."

Be there without being asked.
Do things that make people happier—and cost you nothing.
Smile, hold a door, pay a compliment.

Be open without obligation
...and no whining.
Whining steals energy from you and others.

You will fail—many times.
Just point yourself in the direction of better,
And take as many steps as you can
Every day.

FINAL THOUGHTS

Grace. The catalyst for the greater good, greater connection, the greater kinship.

Think with grace.
Put thoughts of others first.
Patience in being and doing.

See with grace.
Look for ways to help.
Do not wait to be asked.

Listen with grace.
Let other voices be heard.
Wait your turn to speak.

Hear with grace.
Pay attention to what is said.
And what is not.

Speak with grace.
Welcome others.
Use words that affirm others.

Charm with grace.
Put people at ease.
Smile. Speak. Laugh.

Lead with grace.
Turn I into we.
Them into us.

Honor grace.
See. Listen. Hear.
Speak. Charm. Lead.
Think. Always.

Grace. Forever.
And always.

HOW TO USE THESE POEMS AND STORIES

This collection of poems is intended to provoke reflection about what leadership is and is not. Some poems and stories typify the ugliness we see around us. More, however, depict what it means to lead others when times are tough. Leaders are those who apply what they know to help others succeed. They are not altruists per se; they are practical women and men who see their role as making a positive difference.

So, pick a poem or a series of poems and reflect on them.

- *What do these poems / stories say about us?*

- *What insights into yourself do they reveal?*

- *How might you change how you think and act when it comes to making the choices that matter most?*

If you wish to go deeper, consider these questions.

- *How much energy do I expend in proving my point rather than listening to others?*

- *How well do I regard colleagues with whom I disagree?*

- *Why do I like to think of myself as being better than everyone else?*

- *How well did I pay attention to what my spouse told me this morning?*

- *What can I do better tomorrow and the next day to bring out my better self?*

The answers you give are yours. You may wish to share your thoughts with others who have read the same poems. It doesn't matter that you agree. What matters is that you express yourself and, in doing so, connect with others in ways that illuminate what makes us what and who we are. Human!

ACKNOWLEDGMENTS

This collection of poems and stories would not have taken shape without the help of Davin Salvagno of Maison Vero. There was another book I had in mind, but Davin's counsel steered me toward putting my leadership thinking into verse.

Thanks go to Scott Jeffrey Miller of Gray + Miller, the talent agency cum artist fulfillment center. Scott is a prolific author who has been referred to – reverentially mind you – as "a marketing machine." Something we authors need so desperately.

I also want to thank Alan Mulally, former CEO of Boeing Aircraft and Ford Motor Company, for his wise counsel about all things involving leadership and grace. Garry Ridge, chairman emeritus of the WD-40 Company, has been a kind teacher to me, as well as a friend and supporter. Sarah McArthur deserves a shout-out for being in my corner as an editor and friend for more than twenty years.

Marshall Goldsmith, whom I first met in 2004, has been a strong presence in my life as a friend, mentor, and creator of 100 Coaches. Becoming a member of this group has been the best thing to happen to me in my late career. The colleagues I have met and the friends I have made me wiser. Special thanks go to Brenda Bence, Alaina Love, Sally Helgesen, Cynthia Burnham, Rhett Power, Suzy Burke, Eddie Turner, Greg Williams, Terry Jackson, Ken Pasternak, and so many more whose forgiveness I ask for failing to note their support.

And no acknowledgment would be valid without noting the support and patience and love my wife, Gail, has granted me—year after year, decade after decade… for nearly a half-century.

ABOUT JOHN

John Baldoni is an internationally recognized keynote speaker, senior communications advisor and author of 15 books translated into ten languages.

John's thought leadership is reflected in his writing and choice of media: columns, videos, and books. He also integrates piano improvisations into his keynotes, which he illustrates with his still-life photos. John also authored three collections of poetry.

From 2020 to 2025, John hosted LinkedIn Live's *GRACE under pressure* interview series. This platform has enabled him to interview more than 250 global business, academic, and thought leaders and doers.

John is also a member of 100 Coaches, a select group of business, science, medicine and coaching thought leaders founded by Marshall Goldsmith.

John's newest venture is the Baldoni ChatBot, an AI tool that uses John's database of books, articles and videos to provide virtual answers to management and leadership questions.

John's leadership resource website is <u>www.johnbaldoni.com</u>.

Representing a community of authors whose books have collectively sold hundreds of millions of copies, the founders of The Gray + Miller Agency launched Maison Vero, a professional publishing house that partners with rising authors to bring their thought leadership to the world. Our representation covers every aspect of thought leadership, including U.S. senators, governors, and ambassadors, billionaire founders and entrepreneurs, researchers, academics, scientists, consultants, practitioners, social influencers, C-suite leaders, adventurers, professional athletes, artists, and creators. We partner with thought leaders and world changers like you who have a story to tell. By bringing decades of professional expertise to our clients, we are charting a new path in a timeless industry that transcends publishing norms, transforming powerful thoughts into impactful books that inspire minds, ignite hearts, and open doors.

Visit maisonvero.com to view our growing list of authors, or to submit a proposal for publication consideration.

Follow Maison Vero for insight and inspiration on social media:

 MaisonVero  MaisonVero MaisonVeroPublishing

For information about special discounts for bulk purchases, please call 1-949-333-4872 or email info@graymilleragency.com.

Maison Vero is a partner brand of The Gray + Miller Agency, a speaking, literary, and talent consortium. For more information on the talent represented by The Gray + Miller Agency, or to bring any of our thought leaders to your organization or live event, please visit our website at graymilleragency.com.